Dena,

Thank you so m[uch]
for your early suppo[rt]
and belief in me from th[e]
beginning.

Blessings,
Craig Arthur

Feeling Alive Again!

The Outsider's Guide to Conquering Depression

Craig Arthur

Copyright © 2019 by Craig Arthur

All rights reserved. No part of this book may be reproduced or used in any manner, graphic, electronic, or mechanical, recording, taping, or by any information storage retrieval system without written permission of the author except for the use of quotations in critical articles and reviews.

First paperback edition August 2019

Edited by Mary Ann Tate

Cover photographs and design by Moch Media
(www.mochmedia.com)

ISBN 978-0-359-23094-5 (paperback)

Disclaimer

The information provided in this book is designed to provide helpful information on the subjects discussed. This book is not meant to be used, nor should it be used, to diagnose or treat any medical condition. For diagnosis or treatment of any medical problem, consult your own physician. The publisher and author are not responsible for any specific health or allergy needs that may require medical supervision and are not liable for any damages or negative consequences from any treatment, action, application or preparation, to any person reading or following the information in this book. References are provided for informational purposes only and do not constitute an endorsement of any websites or other sources. Readers should be aware that the websites listed in this book may change.

This book is not designed for emergency situations. If you are experiencing thoughts of suicide and have intentions to act, seek help immediately.

Call the national suicide hotline: +1 (800) 273-8255

Or visit the website here: https://suicidepreventionlifeline.org/.

Table of Contents

Acknowledgements	2
Introduction	4
Chapter 1: Hell on Earth	7
Chapter 2: Your Quest Begins Here	14
Chapter 3: Convention Crumbles	19
Chapter 4: Nature IS Nurture	27
Chapter 5: The Water of Life	33
Chapter 6: You Are What You Eat, Eats	40
Chapter 7: Recess for Adults	45
Chapter 8: En Light En Ment	56
Chapter 9: The Healing Powers of Earth	68
Chapter 10: Hygiene as Nourishment	75
Chapter 11: Seeking Holistic Care	80
Conclusion	88
Resources:	91

Acknowledgements

To my parents Sally and William and my Aunt Lenore who have demonstrated unconditional love to me over the course of my 40 years. Words will never have the ability to express the deep gratitude I have for you. Despite my many trials and tribulations, expressions of anger and blame, and years of suicidal depression, you never abandoned me. You always were a source of hope and support and have forgiven me for countless errors. You accepted me each step of my unconventional path to discovering freedom, well-being, and wholeness.

To Robert, or "Grandpa Bob." You extended funding to me at the creation moment of this project. You are someone who lives to support others in any way that you are able and are very generous with your time and resources.

Jen and Sawyer, you have been with me for nearly every step of this project. Through all the tangents, stalls, and restarts we have grown together. I am honored to be your friend.

To my editor, Mary Ann Tate. Thank you for harmonizing these subjects into the final manuscript through encouragement and refinement of language.

With appreciation, love, and gratitude.

Craig Arthur

Introduction

I am no longer the young man who was diagnosed with a life-long mental illness. I do not take pharmaceuticals for depression or anything else, with the exception of the rare emergency or major injury. Traditional medicine advocates that medication is the answer. I have dedicated the better part of my life to find other solutions, and that is what I am sharing with you here.

I am just one person and I tell of my experience. What follows is just the tip of the iceberg of information that is readily available to you. I will offer just a few of a mountain of resources. You may be surprised at what you find. You are the one in charge of your health and well-being. You have the power to say yes, to say no, and to say how it goes. You must become the advocate for your own vitality.

In this book, I present only a fraction of what is available inside the world of holistic lifestyle choices. It is meant only as an introduction, a beginner's guide, a catalyst for a transformative journey. A quest if you will. My hope is that it empowers you to take charge of your own mental state and overall well-being. This requires one hundred percent personal responsibility for your own health. In addition, it will take time, intention, and deliberate choices moment-by-moment, day-by-day, week-by-week, month-by-month, and year-by-year. My hope is that you will now see depression, not as a debilitating mental illness, but as a signpost of dis-ease in the body and a gateway to vitality.

I am the embodiment of all of the suggestions and practices I cover in this book. I view my own body as an ecosystem and make all decisions with that in mind. I purposely carve out the time to spend in nature as much as possible. I drink and bathe in the purest waters available. I primarily consume pure, whole, and real foods. I have a stable and healthy weight that is proper for my body type so that I can function well and participate in vigorous activities. I practice numerous forms of exercise to keep my body strong and mobile. I meditate often and practice breathing intentionally almost every day so that I can be calm in the face of any storm and be the source of my own inspiration. As often as I can I bond with the sun, taking in the rays of light through my skin and eyes, boosting my immunity and helping me stay youthful. I avoid unnatural sources of light when I am able and protect my eyes with blue light blocking glasses when I can't. I spend time barefoot or in bare skin contact with the earth and sleep on a grounding mat to relieve the inflammation prevalent in modern living. It also has provided the most consistent sleep I have ever known. I have eliminated nearly all conventional hygiene and cleaning products from my home and either replaced them with pure ones or no longer need them at all. I regularly see holistic practitioners to deepen my healing even further and to maintain and increase my vitality and relaxation.

Do I experience depressive thoughts and moods? Absolutely. I own them, I embrace them, and I love them. They are a part of being human and a part of me. They are an indicator to me that I have fallen off of my path. I use them as a signpost to make course corrections in my actions to align with my optimum self. Do the negative thoughts and moods control my actions and my experience? Absolutely not. They are a part of me, but they no longer define me. This is my hope and deepest wish for you.

Chapter 1: Hell on Earth

It's deceivingly heavy, I thought, as I looked at the gun in my hands. It is like the one the cops use on television, black, metallic, and shiny. I hold it in my right hand and put it to my right temple. I repeat the motion with my left hand to the left side of my head. Wait, didn't I hear somewhere that shooting yourself through your open mouth at an upward angle was the most successful way of killing yourself? I could just pull the trigger and release myself from the unending suffering; the pain would stop instantly. I would no longer be a burden to my family and friends. I wouldn't have to go on living in constant mental agony. In one moment, it could all be over. There would be a terrible mess for my family to find. I hear a train rumbling by in the distance. I could jump in front of it. At least then my family wouldn't have to deal with the mess.

For more than a decade these thoughts of suicide were a sanctuary from my suffering. They were the only place I could find peace. If my family had owned a gun, I'd be dead now. If I had not been imprisoned in my home with debilitating depression I could have bought my own gun, and I'd be dead now. If I'd garnered the strength to walk to the railroad tracks, I'd be dead now. If I wasn't surrounded by friends and family who showered me with unconditional love and support, I'd be dead now.

Sometimes, when I am feeling really low, these memories return to me, but I am no longer depressed. There are days when I experience negative thoughts, feelings, and emotions, but I am no longer suicidal. How can this be? How can I go from planning ways to take my own life to not being depressed? Well, one day I made a decision, a decision that would take me on a journey to enlightenment and freedom from depression. I am going to share with you how you too can overcome the darkness of depression and step into the light and start feeling alive again.

I have and had every reason to be depressed and to live my life in isolation, which I did for as long as I could. At age six, my friend's father who lived a few houses away molested me. Between six and eight, I was molested multiple times by the older kids next door who were physically much larger and stronger being in middle and high school. The abuse I received was beyond sexual, as I was sometimes jumped by groups of boys and girls and held against my will for lengths of time and physically harmed. As a boy, my body was violated multiple times and in many ways against my consent. The repression of the anger and helplessness I felt created patterns of survival that led to extreme depression into adulthood.

I lived my life as if I was under constant threat, and other people were never to be truly trusted. Why did I never tell anyone? I grew up in a culture where men were supposed to be tough. They weren't supposed to cry or show emotion. Men didn't express their emotions in that way. Therefore, I kept my mouth shut. Now my opinion is that aspect of our masculinity is backward. To express emotion and speak up about injustice and abuse shows courage. I hope to be an example for all men in this arena. It is ok to be afraid, to tell your stories of abuse, and to cry until the hurt and pain are released.

I began to take on coping mechanisms and self-medicating tendencies, which ultimately fueled years of suicidal depression in my teens and twenties. Isolation from others became a survival technique. Outside of school and activities where I didn't have a choice, I spent most of my time in the absence of other people. I stopped playing with other kids and putting myself in situations where I was exposed to danger, which to me was anywhere at any time. I learned that the combination of junk food and television could numb my emotional turmoil and distract me. My new routine became consuming anything and everything that was sweet and salty and eating way past the point of fullness. As time passed, I spent more and more hours in front of the television watching cartoons and sitcoms but could really zone out to whatever I could find. I would do anything at all to not think and, especially, not feel.

In high school, I found ways to express myself a little bit in safe and comfortable outlets. I veered toward playing sports and being a leader in the church youth group. I managed to have a handful of very close friends, although it took some time and vetting for me to extend that level of trust. I can see now how I never fully gave myself over to anyone or anything and always kept one foot out of the door because eventually, I knew that I'd find a reason not to trust the person or group. Even though I was very interested in girls I found it extremely difficult to make those connections due to social anxiety and only managed one girlfriend for a few months before the age of 18. Those four years offered me a reprieve from the constant hell that was my mental state.

In college, without structure and supervision, I quickly spiraled downward. The few friends I managed to make quickly turned out to be untrustworthy. I made sure of it. As a depressed and angry young man, I can't really blame them for preferring the company of others and judging me. I doubled and tripled down on my overeating of junk food and endless hours of mindless screen time. I learned that alcohol was an excellent way to temporarily release social anxiety and connect with people, especially women, in an altered state. Ultimately though, I was headed for disaster. I gained a tremendous amount of weight as I self-soothed with the temporary relief of junk food. I was embarrassed and ashamed to be seen, leading to more isolation and more depression. I only came out to drink at parties.

Witnessing this, my parents urged me to get help in the best way they knew. At nineteen years old I made my first visit to a psychiatrist. I waited outside the office for what felt like hours. I thought I would be laying down on a couch or chair like in the movies. Instead, I remember going into a dark room with, for some reason, the shades drawn on an already gloomy spring day. There was a doctor in his thirties with glasses and a desk light on. I thought I would be telling him my life story. I thought he'd want to help me to get to the bottom of it. Instead he went through a checklist of simple questions. Are you feeling sad? How often? About how much time do you feel sad vs. happy? The whole experience was very quick, with a generous estimate of 15-20 minutes. After going through his checklist, he explained that he was diagnosing me with depression. It was a life-long illness and there was something inherently wrong with my brain. I had a chemical imbalance and I had been born that way. It wasn't my fault. However, the only way to correct that imbalance was with medication. Pharmaceuticals are tricky, as sometimes they work and sometimes they don't. This was the best that I could hope for. Again, this was a life-long diagnosis that would have to be monitored by a professional, like himself, forever. I could not manage it on my own.

I was indignant as my mind began to run wild. What is this chemical imbalance? I was born with a broken brain? After 15 minutes you've now diagnosed me with a life long illness? I didn't believe him. There was something about this that wasn't right. I was angry, confused, and hopeless. The best I could hope for was a managed life of pills and doctor visits? Life as I knew it was over. I didn't know any other options and doctors were the authorities. It didn't seem right but I also didn't want to be depressed anymore. I didn't want my family to have to deal with my moods either. Lacking alternatives, I took the pills.

For the next four years my depression got progressively worse. I changed colleges four times, never finding what I was looking for in terms of education or a social network. I continued to isolate myself, overeat, drink alcohol more and more often, and distract myself by watching television and movies. I didn't agree with my diagnosis. Yet, I went on and off antidepressant medications as I saw how my moodiness and attitude were having negative repercussions on those around me. The only thing that made some difference was the talk therapy the doctors recommended in addition to the pills. I found a therapist who I was comfortable with. All she really did was listen, but I always left those sessions feeling a bit more hopeful.

My sense of time disappeared. Life became a repeating daily pattern of hell on Earth. I began to avoid everybody, including my family. I stayed up all night eating and watching television. At about four or five in the morning, I would finally go to sleep just as the world began to wake up. I would stay in bed until the late afternoon. When I awoke, I would spend an hour or two in bed, wishing that I had not awakened. I hated being alive and wished for death. That's when I'd think about the gun and killing myself. It offered some temporary relief. The thought of being dead was the most comforting thought I would have that day. When I did finally get up, I'd go straight to laying on the couch, and begin to watch television. My whole life became about avoidance, numbness, and distraction.

At the desperate urging of my family, I entered an outpatient program for mental illness at a hospital. I was twenty-three and peaking at almost two hundred and fifty pounds on a five-foot ten inch frame. I was in the midst of my worst and longest episode of depressive symptoms to that point. I received an upgraded life-long diagnosis of "severe depression." I needed pharmaceuticals to balance my brain chemistry. I was prescribed a new pill along with Cognitive Behavioral Therapy, or CBT, and group therapy sessions. I was devastated, obese, and completely hopeless. The psychiatrist told me that the only way for me to survive was to take medication for the rest of my life.

It was then in group therapy that I observed my peers consuming soft drinks and junk food at each break. There were vending machines everywhere. Most had sedentary habits and were overweight like me. Something was not right. The whole chemical imbalance, born with a broken brain paradigm just didn't make sense to me. I had been a straight A student my whole life and received multiple scholarships to college. Something clicked inside of me. A tiny flame of indignance suddenly became a roaring fire of rebelliousness. In that therapy session I said "NO, there is NOTHING wrong with me. The answers to my dilemma are not here." It was then I decided to pursue a holistic lifestyle that emphasized a healthy body as the gateway to wellness.

Chapter 2: Your Quest Begins Here

As mentioned before, I was diagnosed with depression multiple times in my late teens and early twenties. I tried the conventional way of taking pills to correct a chemical imbalance in my brain. I also tried out a few extreme alternatives, anything to not be depressed. By my mid-twenties, I was one hundred pounds overweight. I was debilitated from years of wasting my life away on the couch, hypnotized by a screen and, wishing I was dead.

After a few years of the conventional approach, I said, "No!" to the whole born with a broken brain paradigm. I have spent the last 20 years researching and implementing solutions to this dilemma of depression. I have the advantage of seeing this issue from way outside the box, and from the patient's point of view. I had had enough of doctors and experts in the field telling me what was wrong. Most had never experienced it themselves. The conventional approach said I had a chemical imbalance in my brain that could be alleviated with pharmaceuticals and talk therapy. I am not a proponent of treating depression with conventional diagnoses or medications.

For the rest of this book, I request you take on an attitude of openness so you may receive information freely. Have an attitude of hope, because it's likely that the solutions to your issues are here or that this book will point you in the right direction for assistance. Some information may be brand new and possibly not easy to read. Be gentle, be open, and receive.

What exists in the pages of this book is a new paradigm for how you can view depression—not as a diagnosable mental illness but as a messenger from your body that something is seriously out of whack. You will learn to see depression as the gateway to optimum health should you choose the route I am laying out for you. You will learn that most depression is the symptoms of imbalances of the body and nourishment deficiencies. The Standard American Diet, or S.A.D., has been at the root of many health issues. I now expand the concept to what I call the Standard American Lifestyle, encompassing our conventional way of living these days. You will learn that there is indeed nothing "wrong" with your brain, and there never was a chemical imbalance unless you began taking an antidepressant medication. You will learn a variety of lifestyle solutions to harmonize yourself with nature and alleviate depressive symptoms.

We are in the middle of an epidemic of mental illness, and the time for a new way is now. According to the World Health Organization, depression is now the number one illness in the world. You will not find a quick fix here. What you will find is the culmination of my life's work to help you find your true self, maybe for the first time. I am giving you the keys to the kingdom of well-being, which I assert is your birthright. All the information is available for all to seek for themselves outside of this book. I have simply compiled it here.

Depression and negative thoughts are a natural part of the human experience. You are supposed to feel sad or worse when somebody close to you dies, or you break up with your partner, or a traumatic event occurs. These feelings, emotions, and thoughts are meant to come and go like a current. When the body, mind, and spirit are healthy, they flow through at a natural pace that is unique to your character. However, when depression becomes chronic that is the indicator that something needs to be adjusted. When there is a block in the flow of well-being, a course correction needs to be made. For me, it usually begins in the body.

I make no promises that you will never experience depressive thoughts, moods, and episodes again in your lifetime. As with me, this may be a pattern of yours. It doesn't mean that there is anything wrong or that you are broken and need to be fixed. Consider that you are whole and complete just as you are. Your depression is simply an indicator that your body is not functioning optimally.

I am here to empower you, first by providing hope, and then with information. I will also give you strategies and methods for implementing a variety of techniques in your daily life. You are in charge now. You have the power inside you to not only leave the depression behind, but also to discover a whole new level of health you would have never dreamed available.

You are responsible for your well-being. In order to achieve the kind of results I am talking about, you must be the one ultimately responsible. Not your doctor, not your psychiatrist, not anybody except you. You are responsible to get yourself out of the pit of despair. To be clear I am not saying that you have to do it alone. Absolutely not. In fact, I will recommend how you must rely on the help and assistance of others to make these kinds of changes, especially if you'd like to experience actual results.

A new way involves lifestyle choices that will allow your body and mind to begin functioning again, as they were intended to. A new way involves being responsible moment to moment for the choices that you make. The new way will involve taking baby steps forward and sometimes falling down flat on your face. The new way will also give you the strength to get back up. The new way involves responsibility, choice, and action. What you do with your physical body determines the level of your health.

For the rest of this book, I will address the following holistic lifestyle topics:

- human nature as it was designed
- pure water
- nourishing your body through food choices
- movement that is fun and playful
- the benefits of sunshine
- connecting physically with the earth
- switching to truly natural personal hygiene products

- connecting with holistic practitioners

By reading this book, you are embarking on a quest. No more cures for disease. Instead, holistic lifestyle choices that allow your body to function optimally. With a healthy body and access to your own vital energy, debilitating depression is simply not possible. I offer you choices and actual tools to master your mood. Please read this book at the pace that suits you. Take on the suggestions gently and over time. Take baby steps one by one to alleviate debilitating depressive symptoms once and for all. Experience for yourself the wondrous changes to the body, mind, and spirit.

Chapter 3: Convention Crumbles

The conventional approach, or modern allopathic medicine, to depression is a fallacy. *Allopathic* medicine, or *allopathy*, is a term that refers to science-based, modern medicine, such as the use of medications or surgery to treat or suppress symptoms or the ill effects of disease. My assertion, based on the research and work of others, as well as my own experience, is that it is a fabrication. I am not alone in this way of thinking, as many types of professionals, including psychiatrists, bolster my opinions. This allopathic western way continues by conventionally trained professionals who learned their knowledge inside of a broken system. It is also designed to bolster the large pharmaceutical companies. It's really that simple. This story unfolds in the pages of the book *Psychiatry Under the Influence: Institutional Corruption, Social Injury, and Prescriptions for Reform*, by investigative journalist Robert Whitaker and Lisa Cosgrove.

In this book, the authors claim that people and companies with motives invented the diagnoses for depression and most mental illnesses. They were created and expanded upon by psychiatry, a field of medicine that was looking for a way to make itself legitimate in the early 1900s. Psychiatry had been the laughing stock of medicine. In order to be credible and respected, they created a bunch of problems to solve. The original and subsequent antidepressant drugs do not work and never have, according to the research of Whitaker and

Cosgrove. Yet, western medicine continues to create and push these drugs on the masses to this day. The evidence suggests that not only do these drugs not work any better than a placebo but can potentially cause long term harm and dependence in that they might even cause a chemical imbalance in your brain. The only exceptions for the use of mind-altering pharmaceuticals are in extreme cases. Even then, they should be used only in the short term.

I am not able to cover this whole story in detail here. If you want to delve deeper into this topic, I highly suggest you read the book yourself and make your own choice about what to think. I have experienced the pills and psychiatric methods for myself. Now, I embody my own holistic remedies and solutions. I will, however, offer you some of the story in the words of others. Take a look at what the experts say, below, and decide for you.

> Our society thinks of medicine as a noble pursuit, and thus it expects a medical profession to rise above financial influences that might lead it astray. The public expects that medical researchers will be objective in their design of studies and their analysis of the data; that the results will be reported in an accurate and balanced way; and that the medical profession will put the interests of the patients first. However, in recent years, there has been a steady flow of reports, both in the mainstream media and in academic journals, detailing the corrupting influence that pharmaceutical money has had on modern medicine. {3}

During the past 35 years, psychiatry has transformed American culture. It has changed our view of childhood and what is expected of "normal" children so much so that more than 5 percent of school-age youth now take a psychotropic drug daily. It has changed our behavior as adults, and in particular, how we seek to cope with emotional distress and difficulties in our lives. It has changed our philosophy of being, too, as we have come to see ourselves as less responsible for ourselves, and instead more under the control of brain chemicals that may or may not be in "balance." Our use of psychiatric medications could even be said to range from womb to grave: an increasing number of infants born today are exposed to an antidepressant in utero, and psychiatric drugs are regularly given to the elderly in nursing homes to individuals without psychiatric disorders. {7}

The American Psychiatric Association (APA) and the larger institution of psychiatry, in collaboration with the pharmaceutical industry, publicly promoted the "understanding" that psychiatric disorders were caused by a chemical imbalance in the brain, and that psychiatric drugs helped fix that imbalance, like "insulin for diabetes." American society as a whole came to understand that was true, and, as millions of Americans can attest, that was the message told by psychiatrists (and other prescribing physicians) to individual patients. {157}

The findings of Whitaker and Cosgrove show that as far back as the early 1970s, the chemical imbalance theory began to fall apart in multiple studies. Yet, the American Psychiatric Association continues to promote antidepressants as a treatment for depression to this day. When examined closely, numerous studies reveal the medications do not provide any measurable benefit and actually even cause harm. Their conclusion: Taking medication for any kind of psychiatric condition makes you worse off in the long term. Better to never take an antidepressant or any other kind of mood-altering medication.

It's totally fine to be in shock right now. This could be a bombshell to you and the first time you ever heard anything like this. I urge you to open yourself up to a whole new paradigm for life. Say goodbye to diagnoses and life-long illnesses due to so-called chemical imbalances in the brain. Holistic lifestyle choices are the course correction you've been seeking. Prepare yourself for increasing experiences of well-being, however that occurs to your own unique life.

Maybe you are perfectly happy with what's working for you, taking your pills and seeing your doctor for maintenance every three months. You like the quick fix approach that breaks us into parts and pieces and tries to address individual chemicals in the brain. What I will say is, from what I've researched and what I have experienced, the long-term prognosis for the conventional approach is not good.

Why listen to me? Because, if you don't you will get more of the same. The latest pill as the supposed "cure" for depression. New medications to keep you managed. More doctor visits. More suicides.

More depression. More, more, more. I see some signs that modern medicine is catching on. With the Internet and the free flow of information these days, more and more people will choose another way. We are at the forefront of a total revolution of health care from top to bottom. Preventative medicine comes from a lifestyle in harmony with nature. The opposite approach, the denial of nature, has not and will not work. It is the root of all illness.

There is no one answer to your depression dilemma. The simple strategy is to mimic nature in as many ways as possible. Do we have to give up all the conveniences of modern life? No. I think that some of the same things that doom us are the same things that will ultimately redeem us. What I am presenting here is the holistic lifestyle choices approach to living as the remedy for most depressive symptoms. We can compensate for the weakening of the species by using strategies bringing nature back into every aspect of life. Nature provides all of the keys to not only conquering depression once and for all but for optimum well-being & vitality, as well.

Hope is a wonderful feeling. A glimpse of hope can defeat the most debilitating depression and soul-sucking anxiety, one moment at a time. All you have to do is let go and try on a new viewpoint. Please take on the suggestions gently. Experience for yourself the wondrous changes to the body, mind, and spirit. Over time, you will have many tools to alleviate depressive symptoms. Will the symptoms ever be one hundred percent eradicated? Likely not. What you will get is a healthy body that is a foundation for mental and emotional health to flourish. This is a new way.

You might be angry. You might be angry with me. You might be angry at the current conventional methodology for the way it is used to diagnose and treat depression. You might be confused right now. Maybe you've accepted conventional methods or have never even thought there were alternatives. You may have never heard of any of this. You may be feeling hopeless and that you can't continue. The path may appear too long and too hard. Many of these emotions and feelings can be broken down into fear. I know that fear of the unknown can stop you from moving forward. I am well aware of fear involved with leaving behind what's known and what's easy.

But what about my doctor? What about the whole field of psychiatry? We have been taught that doctors are infallible. We have been taught that they are all experts in their field. Don't they go to school for years for their methods? We have been taught to obey the people in the white coats. Well, that's all very valid. For a long time, I was angry with psychiatrists and doctors in general for the way the current paradigm is. I was mad at the whole medical industry for the treatment I received. As I researched and discovered my suspicions true, I wanted to fight everyone who disagreed with me. Every time I was put in a situation where a doctor was making a decision about my family members or me I wanted to fight. I wanted to make them all wrong. I wanted to call them all stupid. Why could they not hear me?

I have come to terms with the fact that the practitioners themselves are not out to get me. I know that the majority of doctors and psychiatrists truly want to help their patients. I no longer blame the individuals. I have no more time for anger towards the opinions of others or their choices to be closed off to the mountain of evidence against conventional ways. I didn't want to believe it either.

The new way involves lifestyle choices that will ALLOW your body and mind to begin functioning again as intended. The new path involves being responsible moment to moment for the choices that you make. The new way will involve baby steps forward and sometimes falling down flat on your face. The new way will also give you the strength to get back up. The new way involves responsibility, choice, and action.

I am here to empower you. I first want to provide hope, and then to empower you with information. I will also give strategies and methods for implementing a variety of techniques in your daily life. You are in charge now. You have the power inside of you to not only leave the depression behind, but also to discover a whole new level of health you would have never dreamed available. That is the purpose of this book. You are in the driver's seat now.

You are responsible for your own well-being. In order to achieve the kind of results I am talking about. You must be the one ultimately responsible. Not your doctor, not your psychiatrist, not anybody but you. You are responsible to get yourself out of the pit of despair. To be clear I am not saying that you have to do it alone. Absolutely not. In fact, I will be saying over and over that you must rely on the help and assistance of many to make these kinds of changes, especially if you'd like to see actualized results.

"It turns out that everything we've come to know as fact about our health turns out to be no more than wild conjecture. Conjecture that has no science to support it. Conjecture that, to some people, made sense."

"Not anymore." (Wiley 24)

To research my claims for yourself and to draw your own conclusions, I suggest reading the following books (One already mentioned above):

1) *Psychiatry Under the Influence: Institutional Corruption, Social Injury, and Prescriptions for Reform*, by Robert Whitaker and Lisa Cosgrove

2) *A Mind of Your Own: The Truth About Depression and How Women Can Heal Their Bodies to Reclaim Their Lives*, by Kelly Brogan MD, with Kristen Loberg

Chapter 4: Nature IS Nurture

As human beings, we live in an upside-down world. We live outside the rules of nature, almost in contempt of nature itself. This is what I call the *humanscape*. We have been taught to believe that humans are better than the animals and plants around us because of our large brains and our ability to create almost whatever we can fathom. The issue is that our smarts and technology have weakened us as a species. Is there one proven person on the planet who can live like an animal? One that has the strength to live with no clothes, no shelter, and no tools -- like an animal? Is there one person who can match the pound for pound power of an animal and thrive with only the body itself? The answer is a resounding no. Not even indigenous people alive today can survive without tools, clothing, shelter, etc. Our species, even the strongest of us, has long since left the simplicity and strength, albeit unpredictability, of nature. The *humanscape* is the cause of all modern illnesses. Our intelligence cannot come up with a cure for depression because there is none. It is not a disease that can be pinpointed to chemicals in the brain.

Why will the allopathic, or conventional, approach to depression never work? The allopathic approach breaks the body down into parts and pieces. Then it attempts to fix the whole body by correcting the part of piece, a miniscule portion of the puzzle. The chemical imbalance theory for depression is based on one neurotransmitter in the brain, Serotonin. Conventional psychiatrists and doctors, or allopaths, believe that a pill which corrects serotonin in the brain can fix your depressive thoughts This again points to that something is wrong and needs to be fixed. What is totally missed is that 95% of serotonin is produced in your guts, not your brain. You may have never heard that before. Are you now beginning to see why targeting only the brain won't work?

It is my assertion that well-being and vitality are your birthright and part of the natural flow of life for a human being. In order to claim this right, you must live as human beings are designed. To thrive, we must mimic how we are in Nature. As animals ourselves, we are designed to live in community, and we are also an ecosystem within ourselves. Let me explain.

First, in his book, *The Depression Cure: The 6-Step Program to Beat Depression Without Drugs*, Stephen S. Ilardi, PhD, states that isolation is one of the biggest factors associated with depression. People lacking fulfilling connections with others have a high tendency towards being depressed. This can be exacerbated by life stress, which makes us withdraw even further. This, in turn, becomes a difficult pattern to break leaving us seemingly with no way out and nowhere to turn. Ilardi emphasizes that our natural inclination to connect is engraved in our DNA. It is an ancient drive for the stability of shared resources and safety in numbers. The comfort we receive from connection with others cannot be overlooked.

Just as there is a herd of deer, a pack of wolves, a pod of dolphins, or an army of ants, we also have a group name. That name is Tribe. We are community-oriented animals called a tribe of humans. To deny this is to deny our nature, which is to deny ourselves access to optimum well-being and vitality. Due to my traumatic childhood events, I isolated myself for years. Even with holistic lifestyle choices, there was always something important that was missing. Without a connection to other people on a regular basis, we will never achieve optimum well-being. I would never have achieved the level of health that I have today without my community.

New science looks at the human being as an ecosystem. It calls this ecosystem the microbiome. Of the trillions of cells that you think are you, about 90% of them are NOT human cells. The you that you think you are is actually not really much of you at all. In an ecosystem, it takes all the different players for health and stability. Think of the African savannah. Everything is important for the health of the ecosystem from the large dominant predators like the pride of lions, to the herbivores like the gazelles and zebras and water buffalo. Then the plants that the herbivores eat, to the soil which grows the plants, to the healthy bacteria and other keepers of the soil, and so on and so forth down the line are all a part of the ecosystem. What happens when humans arrive and begin to kill off all of the lions for trophies and sport? There are too many grazers who eat all of the grass, and then they run out of food and die off, and so on down the line. Our human intervention destroys the natural flow.

There is a community alive within you. The cutting edge of science and health is labeling this community the microbiome, which includes a variety of bacteria and other microorganisms that live in harmony with you. In her book, *Renegade Beauty: Reveal and Revive Your Natural Radiance*, author Nadine Artemis says that of the 130 trillion cells that comprise the human body, only 30 trillion of those are human cells. You yourself are an ecosystem. There is no way around that. These organisms are your allies in health. Their job is to keep the ecosystem, the host, you, flourishing. Your job is to harmonize with the needs of the ecosystem. There are also unfriendly bacteria and microorganisms that leave you in disharmony, for example, depression. Unfortunately, the *standard American lifestyle* is harming the microbiome. More on that as we move along.

The *standard American lifestyle* and *humanscape* can destroy your ecosystem. You are a community and must be the caretaker of all the organisms that coexist within you. If you don't, things get out of hand pretty quickly. Just as we must operate as a tribe, you can also see that you are your own community within yourself, with numerous organisms living in harmony with you. The goal of the tribe is to thrive and flourish. By taking on a few or all of the things I mention in this book, so you, too, will thrive and flourish as an individual community and as a part of your tribe of choice. This is a new way, which also happens to be a very old one. We are integral parts of the world and are, ourselves, host to a harmonious flourishing community.

There is an innate knowing within us that nature itself is a healer. There are countless studies from all over the globe showing that spending time in nature elevates our mood. The Japanese have shinrin-yoku, or forest bathing, where one takes a stroll through or spends quiet time in the woods. In western society, we have the scientific term biophilia, or the urge to associate with other forms of life, which relieves stress and boosts mood. However you want to define it, we are a part of this world and meant to interact with nature itself on a regular basis. Our modern lives are a far cry from our hunting and gathering days, and cities and towns are full of loud noise and artificial light. We have isolated ourselves from the wild species of the world, and some of us spend little time amongst them. When we relax in a natural setting and interact with the wild things in which we share our world, we expose/reveal the proven elevator of mood and natural reliever of stress. We are designed for it. Accepting that and dedicating time and action towards it can be just the remedy for depression you've been craving. Nature is nurture, and it is the key to your relief and vitality.

Sidebar #1: Letting Go

You will never achieve perfection, the perfect life, and the absence of all so-called negative thoughts, feelings, and emotions. In his book, Letting Go: The Pathway to Surrender, David R. Hawkins, MD, and PhD outlines a process that can offer relief and release from any circumstance. All of us experience negative thoughts, feelings, and emotions at one time or another. When one is depressed, these can seem inescapable and insurmountable. What is even worse is when we resist these experiences because of our preconceived notions that the thought, feeling, or emotion is wrong, to begin with. We believe that negativity is wrong and is to be avoided at all costs. Then, we ourselves are wrong if we have negativity in us. Negativity itself is a form of resistance. When we resist the presence of the negative, then we are resisting resistance. To let go we must first accept and acknowledge the unwanted thought, feeling, or emotion without judgment. It's just there, no right or wrong. Now we are no longer resisting resistance (negativity). Next, after a brief period of time in which we surrender to the negative thought, feeling, or emotion, with intention, we let it go. Is it that easy? Well, yes and no. I personally find it more effective to deal with the feelings inside my body versus each individual thought. And sometimes we must let go of the same thing over and over again until it's finally gone. Perhaps certain aspects of ourselves never go away completely. And, access to letting go is always free and simple. Want to be free? Let it go, surrender, let it go.

Chapter 5: The Water of Life

After a few years of holistic lifestyle choices my depressive symptoms waned and my moods stabilized somewhat. Life-long dreams of adventure became a reality and travel became my new outlet for experiencing the greater world. At age 26 I went to New Zealand and ended up spending the better part of three years there. The first place I lived in was a small town called Wanaka. Nestled underneath majestic mountains and next to a large freshwater lake, it is absolutely gorgeous. Although I was working a winter ski season, the weather in town was downright pleasant during the day. The transportation to work was a couple of miles from the house where I rented a room, and, sometimes, I would walk the distance. One day my Dutch roommate mentioned that there was a natural spring running along the side of the road on the walk home from town. He talked a little about the taste and quality of spring water and how it provided an energizing effect. In addition to the purity, it just tasted and felt good he said.

The next day I stopped at the spring on my way home to take a drink. The spring was coming out of the rocks through a narrow pipe about a foot off the ground and ran into a ditch where it flowed away down the street and into the lake. I bent over and took my first sip right from the moving water itself. It was cold and tasted pure and refreshing. Almost immediately, I felt my energy and mood shift and started smiling. I knew I liked doing this, for certain. For the rest of my stay in that town, I made it a habit to stop by as often as possible. I would drink as much as I could and fill up a bottle to take home with me and finish the rest of the day. This was the beginning of my journey with pure water.

Our earth is comprised of approximately 70% or more of water give or take. Human beings are made up of an equal percentage. We are children of the earth. This is undeniable. If we were made up of mostly water, then wouldn't our interaction with water have great importance? Our equal percentage is no coincidence and should be enough to communicate to take water more seriously.

I have almost unlimited access to clean potable water, you might say. While supposedly free of germs, most municipal water is not pure. The average glass of tap water in America is primed with at least two substances that are not beneficial for us – chlorine and fluoride. The notion that we are drinking the best water is a fallacy. It might even be the very thing that is contributing to your depressive symptoms.

Tap water contains chlorine because it is an antibiotic. Antibiotic simply means anti-life. It is inserted into our water to get rid of harmful micro-organisms. Being indiscriminate, it also destroys beneficial micro-organisms. Look back at the microbiome mentioned in "Chapter 3: Nature is Nurture". What do you think happens to your ecosystem when you are drinking antibiotics with every sip of water? It damages your fragile community. What do you think happens when you do that day in and day out for your whole life? Unless you frequent natural springs, you have never known a day of your life without your body having to compensate for an ailing microbiome. What happens to the river or ocean when there is an oil spill? The animals get all covered with oil and the ecosystem either dies, gets sick, or suffers greatly. But what happens over time? Nature always comes back to heal itself if left alone long enough. News flash. All of the chemicals and oils do the same thing to you that they do if dumped in a river or stream. It screws up the environment very badly.

How did we get to a place where water is sterile and full of chemicals? Well, we have to thank Louis Pasteur for his germ theory. When you hear the word, bacteria, what is your reaction? Most people I know cringe because of our fear of germs. Some bacteria are good. Labeling these micro-organisms under the blanket that they are all bad has left us fearful. Sterilize our world. Sterilize your homes. Sterilize the water. At what cost? The unwanted bacteria that cause disease and illness are those that can only succeed in a weak ecosystem. They exist to prey on your weakness. We try to eradicate these things. In reality, they are our partners, with each organism having a right to life. With a healthy human, these things stay in balance and you won't get sick as often.

Does a bog not coexist in the middle of a forest? Does it not need its own special conditions? Does not the forest exist on the mountain or in the desert? I think you get the point. Our stomach is a part of our organs which are a part of our body which is a part of the environment we live in which is a microclimate on the earth. As soon as you accept this without being a germaphobe about it, you will understand that the keys to the kingdom of health come from tending to the microbiome, or your own living-breathing ecosystem in which you already exist.

The story goes that fluoride was put in the water to prevent cavities. According to some, it's a fact that the addition of fluoride is necessary and good for us. Among others, including myself, the benefits and costs of adding fluoride are still a discussion to be had. I think it is not a good thing at all. What is not up for debate is that fluoride in any amount is a neurotoxin. That means that fluoride affects the functioning of your brain. The brain is the all-star organ of focus in our society, and yet we regularly consume a chemical additive that keeps it from performing optimally.

I am simply touching the surface of this topic for you. You may already be rethinking your drinking habits. But what about bathing? The skin is the largest organ in the body, and it is very porous and ventilated. Anything that touches your skin absorbs into your body. When you bathe in tap water, you expose yourself to chlorine and fluoride. You likely shower in and cook with water from the tap daily, as well. The same principles apply.

What does this have to do with depression? Trying on a holistic viewpoint we must look at how to allow the entire body to function optimally. By removing a daily dose of antibiotics from our drinking and bathing water, I think our bodies come back into natural homeostasis in that area. Also, by not taking in another substance that is known to harm brain function, then our brains will start to function better, too. It is simple logic. When your body is allowed to function in a more optimal state, then your moods and thoughts will improve naturally. When harmful additives do not hinder you, then you will function better and be happier.

How do you go about this simple yet effective shift in your water habits? The answer is to invest in one or more high-end filters. One of the best filters is called reverse osmosis. This kind of filter is so effective that it ends up producing water that is nearly sterile. It is not only free of micro-organisms but also free of helpful minerals too. With this type of filter, I recommend adding an organic mineral complex back to your drinking water. In this way, you mimic how water would be found in nature without the harmful bacteria and without chlorine or fluoride. There are also high-end alkaline filters that not only remove the unwanted stuff but also control the PH balance of your water. The jury is still out on the benefits of this type of filter, and, in my experience, they are great as well. Many filters you find, especially cheap ones, usually do not take out the unwanted additives and only alter the taste. These are essentially useless for what we are after here. Make certain you get one that removes the chemicals.

Bottled water in plastic is also not recommended. Water is one of the most powerful substances on Earth, over time able to shape stone and form canyons. Water begins to leach whatever materials were used to form the container almost immediately. Your body having to cleanse these synthetic additives affects your natural flow of well-being, which in turn leads to mood alteration.

As for a shower filter, I recommend getting a type that radically reduces chlorine and fluoride by up to 99%. No filter can take it all out, unfortunately--not one I have seen, anyway. The one that I have actually alters the molecular structure of the water to mimic living flowing river water. It is run through a thin copper tube and spiraled as well as put through a lot of pressure and minerals. The difference I experience is a reduction in the dry skin and dry hair effect post-bathing. I don't shower as much as I used to do. I don't find it as necessary with holistic lifestyle choices because I don't smell or sweat as much anymore. I have replaced ninety percent of my showering with dry brushing. I purchased a specifically made brush to remove the dead skin on a regular basis. This mimics how a lot of animals would clean themselves in nature.

Currently, access to beneficial products is at the touch of your fingertips. The filters and dry brush I mentioned can be found and purchased with a simple internet search. Those without handy skills to install can enlist the help of a friend or professional. The cost is well worth the effort. We are beings of water after all.

Purify the water that goes inside and around you, and your body will purify too. This allows your body to function more optimally, which leads to improved moods and lessening depression. Accept yourself as a being of water in a watery world.

Sidebar #2: Spring Water

The royalty of waters is self-harvested from a natural spring. You can purchase your own testers for mineral contents. Natural springs are found all over the world. Sometimes they are still secret enough to where only the locals know. Some others and I are water nerds and really get into it by making trips to springs to drink our fill and haul as much as we can carry home in glass containers. Those of us in the know drink from glass bottles as much as we can. Note that these natural springs are known to contain live bacteria and often lots of minerals. I have drunk out of more springs more times than anyone I know and have never gotten sick. I have developed a very strong immune system over time and practice.

Chapter 6: You Are What You Eat, Eats

The day I saw the number 244 on the scale I decided, enough is enough. I was an above-average athlete in high school, not an all-star, but above average at most sports. This all changed when I went to college. I already had bad eating habits and they were just covered up by being young and active. There was a term called the "freshman fifteen" referring to students gaining fifteen pounds in their first year of college. It's the weight kids put on when their parents stop feeding them and they get to make all their own choices. Well, I gained twenty pounds in the first semester. I watched as my peers ate similarly and some gained weight while others did not. Clearly, I was more susceptible.

I love the word nourishment. I always ask the question of how will this nourish me? At this moment, what do I need to eat or drink to be nourished? Begin thinking in terms of nourishment. If the old model was to eat this many servings a day to get your proteins, fats, carbohydrates, and all the essential vitamins, then the new way is less is more. The more quality food you eat, the less food you need to eat overall. When you eat to nourish your body and your cells, you will find that the weight comes off or on and that your mood improves drastically.

I offer you a new way to classify food that points you in the right direction to make the best choices. Not in the way it is usually presented to you by measuring portions and counting calories, but perhaps a new way to look at things. Instead, this is a general strategy to always aim for the purest and most nourishing options available in each situation.

First, the bottom of the barrel is what I like to call *dead foods*. This is fast food, almost ALL processed food, AND anything with artificial flavors and/or colors. If you are reading the label and you see unpronounceable chemicals, then it falls in this category. I'm pretty much talking about anything from a large chain supermarket and most major brands. A great example would be most breakfast cereals.

Next, is *conventional whole foods*. Conventional food is the produce (vegetables) and animal products [meat, cheese, milk, butter, etc.] that come from factory farming and industrial farming techniques. This is any type of technique that involves the intentional use of chemical fertilizers, pesticides, fungicides, and herbicides. Also mono-cropping, or growing a single crop on the same piece of land over and over, is employed. When animals are viewed only as a resource then they are typically given hormones and antibiotics to make them grow faster and stay well long enough to harvest. They are also raised under unideal circumstances and fed an unnatural diet. This is factory and industrial farming. If we really get connected to how our food is being produced, we would likely as a collective demand a big change. I hope we are headed in a direction that includes increased respect for the species of animals and plants that we consume.

You are what you eat, AND you are what you eat eats. If the plants are consuming chemicals, then so are you! If the animals are eating those plants and being doped with hormones and antibiotics then so are you! It stays in the food. Conventional food has some value, but the tradeoff for the contaminants they contain doesn't make them worth it to me. Remember, you are consuming everything the animals consume. This option also perpetuates cruelty and suffering to the beings we share this planet with. Unfortunately, most restaurants source their ingredients from this category.

Another category is *organically grown whole foods*. While "Organic" is not a perfect label, it does mean that significantly fewer contaminants and/or drugs have been used in the process. This is the stage where my own health, weight, and mood began to stabilize. I recommend supporting a smaller chain or local health food store when possible. However, even large chain supermarkets are beginning to carry a supply of organic produce and products now.

Even better are *locally & ethically raised foods*. These are not necessarily labeled "organic" but can be. Many farmers do believe in pure food and yet do not want to pay for costly organic certifications. Learn to ask the right questions and most farmers will be honest about their practices. Also, just because they are at the farmer's market do not assume they abstain from using conventional methods. Ask questions like, "Are you certified organic?" If not why? If not what are your methods of growing vegetables or raising animals? You will be able to educate yourself a lot over a short amount of time about how food arrives on your plate. You will also be assured that you are doing your best for your own health and the health of the beings we utilize for our consumption. This is the step of the ladder where your taste buds really begin to open up in the best possible way. I never thought I would crave a bitter green salad, but now I can't get enough.

Nearing the top level, we are at *growing & raising foods*. Imagine your own garden, orchard, greenhouse, or urban farm. Want to eat the best-tasting food in the world and feel amazing? Grow it yourself! Perhaps you can start small with an herb garden. Have a fruit tree? Start eating the fruit! There is a plethora of free information online alone on how to start your own organic gardening.

Reaching the top category now, we are at my favorite, *wild & feral foods*. Did you know that dozens of plants that are considered weeds are actually super nourishing foods and herbal medicines? I gather wild greens for salad and herbs for tea. I have found feral apple trees, wild plums, and peaches. Can you think of anything better than the flavor of truly fresh seafood? Wild and Feral foods contain more nutrients by weight than anything that can be found in any supermarket. Caution! There are also a lot of poisonous plants and fungi. Learn gradually from an expert and be mindful when experimenting with foraging.

In my observations, most people's diets consist of the bottom two groups, *dead & conventional foods*. Perhaps you never before learned of the alternate groups to be explored and consumed. My personal strategy is to always reach for the purest source of food available. By doing so, you can achieve your ideal body and transform your mental state rapidly.

Another sub-category to include often on your plate is fermented food, like kimchi or sauerkraut. They are full of micronutrients and beneficial digestive acids. Also great are available forms of edible fungi, usually in the form of mushrooms, which can be added easily to many meals. I like to eat a lot of varieties of green leaves. The more exotic and flavorful, the better. As the quality and purity of your food increases, you will find previously unknown flavors in items that you used to consider non-palatable. Try steamed beets, roasted radishes, and kimchi with cooked mushrooms and rice. Become friends with vegetables and fruits and build your meals around them. They are no longer a side dish as they are the dish. Prepare for a taste bud explosion and feeling energized and great after a meal instead of bloated and tired.

It is absolutely essential to take what you are eating seriously if you desire to improve your mood. To get more into detail on an ideal diet to eliminate depression, I point you towards Chapter 6: Let Thy Food Be Thy Medicine, or Dr. Brogan's book, *A Mind of Her Own*. She advocates avoiding everything from the lowest groups of nourishment I mentioned. In addition, other foods to avoid include wheat, dairy, corn, sugar, etc., among other things. They cause inflammation and are low in nourishment value. When I focus on sourcing my food from the purest sources, I am generally happy, balanced, lean, and full of energy. Debilitating, un-abating depression cannot touch you when you are nourishing yourself with pure and real food.

Chapter 7: Recess for Adults: DO NOT SKIP THIS CHAPTER!!!

Part A: Moving

In 2011 after four months of doing an at-home fitness craze video series, I was experiencing recurring pain and injury. There was both cardio and weight training, and a lot of it every day of the week. I am certain that lots of people have experienced weight loss and muscle gain in hopes of achieving the "ideal" body using these types of videos. While I did look better, lost weight and gained muscle, I'd also started wearing knee braces for the first time since I had growing pains in high school. After a few months, I could only manage to do the workouts a couple of times a week. This was not the first time I had taken on an extreme exercise challenge trying to reverse my weight and muscle size. However, it would be the last.

The big gym mentality says that in order to be fit you need to always be pushing your body to the limits. New personal goals. You need to do some form of cardio to lose weight and some form of weight lifting to gain muscle. Plus, you are inside under artificial light and breathing circulated air often with artificial chemical smells. A lot of us are even tuned out of our surroundings because we dislike one another so much that we wear headphones or even watch the television in the gym to stay entertained. I haven't entered this kind of facility in a while, but I have been to enough to know the scene. It's a quick fix mentality that has you likely reinforcing improper techniques. For a depressed person, a gym can be a nightmare scenario. Sometimes we loathe ourselves so much it's hard to be around fit people.

I'd wanted to try Tai Chi since reading about the potential benefits in a book about healthy food. I went to the library to do research about it and also checked out a handful of videos on the subject. One video with a focus on back care stood out to me because my lower back was always tight. I had chronic pain that only worsened with all of the push-ups and jump squats. Halfway through the first time trying the video, I was hooked. My back suddenly became looser than it had been in many years. I felt blood flowing and rushing to forgotten places. It was heaven.

I started each morning with a 30- to 60-minute tai chi video. After one month, I had some unbelievable and unexpected benefits. Without altering my diet, I had lost nearly 15 pounds and the entire shape of my body shifted. Since I had put on all of the weight in college, the area of my hips and torso had changed quite a bit. I had developed a slightly more pear-shaped body. Within a month, I had returned to my high school form at my peak. I was shocked in a very good way. This experience led me to start looking way outside the box for making movement more fun and effective.

A variety of sustainable and fun movements is vital to your overall health and well-being. For those suffering from depression or mental illness, it is critical. Exercise is one of the greatest mood shifters known to us. The human species was designed for movement. We are made to walk, run, crawl, climb, jump, swim, manipulate objects, and much more. Depression and a sedentary lifestyle go hand in hand. Those who experience long term depression are very likely under-exercised and lack of variety of movement. Quick fixes and going full blast into a hardcore exercise routine designed for sweeping changes can lead to injuries, pain, and the inability to maintain the frenzied pace. Therefore, we look to our elders, the past, for sustainable movements and ideas have been carried down for the ages.

In yoga there is a concept called beginners mind. Even though it's a routine, you can come to each practice with a mindset as if it were your first time. What could you discover about your own body and movement ability if each time was the first? What if you didn't have opinions about your limits or what you could or couldn't do? You just entered each experience without expectation or limitation. You could avoid pain and injury by gently easing your way into each new modality, stretching your edges slowly and mindfully, being aware of what your state of mind, body, and emotion is each time you practice. Injury is also avoided with a variety of movements. The phrase, "variety is the spice of life," is correct. Variety in your movement is like the flavor that gives your movement diet a good taste and makes you want to cook that meal again and explore new flavors. Some injury and pain don't necessarily have to be avoided at all costs either. They can be good indicators that point out just where your patterns of moving are off and lead to the proper solutions.

Again, I am asking you to take responsibility. There is no one modality to blame if you get injured. You can always say "no" to what is being asked if it is too difficult. You can always modify your exercise to fit what your body can and can't do at the time.

Another lesson you can learn from yoga is that it is a practice. That is the key to a beginner's mind. Even after years of regular yoga practice, I cannot perform the perfect poses pictured in magazines or that are on a friend's social media post. I am not there yet. This is no fad. This is a lifestyle change and an attitude adjustment. One or a combination of the following modalities can assist you in getting to where you want to be. I have seen miracles in my own body. I have also seen the transformation of countless others whose lives have been changed by committing to one of these teachings. Start slow, and here we go.

Qi Gong and Tai Chi are forms of movement based on nature. Both are a series of slow and gentle movements with a focus on breathing and posture. Many of the slow and methodical movements mimic nature in some way and are even named after animals or natural phenomena. This is especially wonderful if you have been sedentary for a while. You do not have to be interested in fighting martial arts to practice Qi Gong or Tai Chi. Classes can be found by searching locally, or you could begin by renting a DVD from the library or even checking for sample videos online. An added bonus is that Tai Chi and Qi Gong are forms of moving meditation. More on meditation later.

Similar to martial arts, there are hundreds of different styles or variations of yoga, which also varies from instructor to instructor. Some of the chain studios streamline their classes. As yoga becomes more westernized, the focus ends up being more on getting a workout, which can be fine. Some styles, such as Kundalini, are quite unique and have tremendous benefits far beyond body improvement. Be curious and courageous here and experiment with what works for you. Your routine will likely change over time as you expand your body and mind through practice. The ultimate goal of yoga is to prepare the body for stillness and meditation through movement. For the complete benefits of a yoga practice, I invite you to try that on.

I began by experimenting at many different studios in my area that offered a free first class, an introductory week, or a discounted first month. I live in the Denver metro area that has a lot of choices. Although yoga is gaining in popularity in the USA, your locale may have far fewer options. I spent a good six months trying out a variety of classes and instructors. Even though I was going to beginner classes, it was very challenging at first. I was determined, though, and forged onward. Eventually, I landed in a comfortable space and found a teacher who taught longer classes, moved through the postures slowly, and emphasized alignment. Luckily, most yoga studios these days are full of average everyday folks, not the stereotypical yogi. Some may utilize meditation and chanting, and you are free to participate in whatever you are comfortable with. Some styles will remind you of cross-fit, and others may seem like taking a nap. I recommend giving a variety a chance.

Vinyasa is a general word that encompasses many styles and is what most people think of when they hear the word yoga. Vinyasa yoga in America usually consists of some sort of flow where you build a routine that goes through a variety of poses that all work together to a culmination point. Remember to take it slow and go at a pace your body is ready for. Some of these poses can be quite difficult and there are always modifications, so please do not be ashamed if you cannot do it right away or even for a while. I've been at it for the better part of a decade, and there are still some poses that I just cannot do. Remember, it's a practice where you always are striving for the ideal but can never reach it. It has direct applications to the rest of your life, and that's why you do it.

Yin yoga is a Chinese style of yoga that focuses on releasing the connective tissue of the body, or fascia. The fascia is the connective tissue of the body that lies underneath the skin but above the muscle. It is like a spider web of interconnected material. Fascia is said to hold traumas of emotional and physical nature. Yin yoga is more static and practiced on the floor with minimal movements. You are encouraged to take a specific shape. Each individual body assumes its own expression of that shape depending on your own mobility. In Yin yoga, you hold a posture for 1 to 3 minutes or even longer when you become more advanced.

Primitive Movement includes crawling, balancing, jumping, running, hanging. These are all things that have been mostly lost in modern times. We sit, we stand, and we walk, all with inefficient posture and form. If you are like me, your formative years were spent on the couch and in chairs, misshaping your spine and curving your head and neck forward. We can practice primitive movement to mimic how we used to navigate through natural environments. The *humanscape* is flat and without obstacles. Crawling is actually frowned upon. We adults don't use the monkey bars and if we do, we get weird looks from concerned parents. In a gym environment it is ok to do pull-ups and dips but what about climbing trees or playing outside. Primitive movement can be practiced from the ground up. Most of us have not been moving in many abstract ways. Basic crawling will make you very tired and stress your body quite a bit. You may find that you don't have to do much at all at first.

When we think of primitive movement, we see people performing amazing feats of agility, strength, mobility, and motion. Before attempting those, we need a foundation that comes from crawling, walking, running, jumping, climbing and carrying objects. I encourage you to focus on proper form versus getting in a sweaty workout. I've tried a lot of exercises. Lifting weights works for some people just fine. For me, lifting weights and doing pushups provides little functional movement. When I began to crawl and roll around on the floor as an adult, I grew stronger and more mobile very quickly. Exercises like Qi Gong or Tai Chi, yoga and primitive movement have you focusing on proper alignment. This gives a good foundation for expanding your abilities. Like a baby, you must crawl before you can walk or run.

In general terms, ecstatic dance is a gathering of human beings who come together for the purpose of dancing only. The ones I attend have a general rule to not have conversations on the dance floor. The focus is on freely expressing your body through the dance itself -- another form of moving meditation. No one is judged for their skills and you don't have to know any dance moves. The only thing to do is express yourself with the music as your guide. This can be one of the most liberating things to do for your body and mind. Dancing is one of the oldest rituals on earth for a reason. We are designed to dance.

Flow arts include hula hoops, climbing, hanging, balancing, swinging, spinning, circus implements, and much more. Moving in a state of flow or learning a new talent can be a fantastic way to motivate oneself to exercise. This is a wonderful and fun way to get fit and increase your movement variety.

Part B: Stillness

Our modern lives are full of constant stimulation. There is no end to the distraction. An often-overlooked form of movement is actually no movement at all. This is stillness or meditation. Almost all ancient traditions have a practice of quieting the mind through either stillness or prayer. The whole point of traditional yoga was to prepare the body and mind for meditation. There is a reason for this. It is common knowledge now, even in western society, that meditation is beneficial for many ailments, including depression. You can become a still observer of the chaotic mind.

I have noticed that people say they can't meditate when in fact they have never tried, or they are trying to achieve some perfect version of it. This, like any exercise or skill, requires practice and consistency. I have been at it for years and have not achieved the status of a monk yet. That's not how it works. Even so, with the benefits of calmness and presence I receive, I doubt I will ever give it up. Guided meditations with a practitioner can be found all over our country currently. Chances are there are at least a few people around you that are leading classes. Search for them through social media, the library, health food store message boards, and by word of mouth. Also, there are many guided meditations to try for free on the Internet with a simple search, especially on YouTube. Your local library likely has some audio meditations available to check out as well.

Another game-changing exercise with very little movement is conscious breathing, sometimes called breathwork. There are many techniques for intentional breathing where it moves from an unconscious act to a conscious one. Flooding the body with air, oxygen, and nitrogen has an invigorating and enlivening effect on the body, mind, and spirit, producing a natural high. Again, conscious breathing classes can now be found in many places. Seek them out. You can also find examples and techniques to try on your own through online searches. Dr. Brogan describes a few examples in her book for deep breathing.

Disclaimer: Never ever use breathing practices while driving or operating heavy machinery. If you are new to this, it can cause you to faint if you go too fast or strong. Please always do this in a safe, comfortable environment.

Moving your body is an essential key to overcoming depression. It is the best natural way to change your state of mind by getting you out of your head and into your body. You cannot achieve optimum well-being without some sort of regular exercise. It simply goes against our design. I highly recommend a variety of gentle and subtle movement practices. Focus and start with one. I do not recommend a serious martial art for the sedentary body, at least not right away. Nor do I recommend any strenuous type of exercise at first. You may get injured and discouraged. Please consult a physician of your choice before beginning any new exercise program. Please enjoy your adult recess.

Sidebar #3: The Wim Hof Method

Wim Hof is a Dutch citizen who is redefining what it means to be human in a public forum. He got his nickname, The Ice Man, by setting a number of records related to cold exposure. His method uses yogic breathing combined with cold-water immersion stimulating dormant abilities to withstand extreme temperatures. His story is quite touching, as he developed his method as a result of his first wife committing suicide and leaving him a widower with children. This tragedy motivated Wim to develop his cold immersion style of therapy as a technique to alleviate depression naturally, by harnessing an inner power he believes we all have within.

Personally, I use the breathing techniques taught by Wim almost every day. Upon awakening, I do multiple rounds of breathwork to energize my body each day and boost my immunity. After purchasing Wim's online course, I have also incorporated cold immersion in water as a regular practice, usually doing it at least once a week, sometimes more. The breathing practice charges me with energy each morning that lasts long into the day. As for the cold immersion, it may sound daunting. I can attest that there is nothing more invigorating than spending five to twenty minutes in a cold Colorado creek. As for natural remedies, I can't think of one that has more instant and noticeable results. It's a game-changer and a state change. I am very happy to have it in my toolbox.

To read more about Wim Hof's story and achievements, to look at the science behind the techniques, and to register for the Wim Hof Method yourself, start here: www.wimhofmethod.com.

Chapter 8: En Light En Ment

Part A: The Risen Savior

During the summers of my college years, I managed to crawl out of the hole of depression for a few months. I traded isolation for beautiful hot weather and sunshine in a more natural setting. I had the privilege of working at a couple of different youth summer camps as a lifeguard in Wisconsin and Minnesota. The community and activity would naturally alleviate crippling depressive symptoms. I would start putting in the work to eat better and less and increase exercise months beforehand to feel comfortable enough to wear a bathing suit in front of others.

My specialties included most water activities like swimming, boating, and water skiing and therefore I was outside by the lake most of the day. For months at a time, I was exposed to the full and direct sun with little shade for many hours at a time. I dutifully put on sunscreen to protect myself and I did manage to avoid sunburn. I was diligent to slather it on at the beginning and end of each morning and evening shift, even having others make certain my back was covered in the places I couldn't reach. That's hundreds of times per summer. Although my skin was as dark brown as it could get, I never got burned.

At the end of the first summer, I developed a discolored rash on my skin. It was small and splotchy and disappeared on its own. The second year, it was significantly larger and took almost a whole year to go away. I avoided dealing with it. The ugly rash added to body shame and only fueled my sadness. After the third summer, the discolored rash covered almost my entire torso and did not go away on its own. It was super embarrassing and ugly, so I finally went to the dermatologist and had it checked out. The diagnosis was called Tinea Versicolor that is a skin rash that grows as a result of an imbalance of microorganisms. It is bacteria that already exist on the skin in a healthy ratio, and when it gets out of balance, it causes a rash. Luckily the cream prescribed at the time worked quickly and effectively. I was told this problem was not necessarily a big deal but was likely to continue on and off my whole life.

I am happy to say that this experience was a catalyst for change that would take me far down a rabbit hole to learn an alternative view of sun exposure. Since then, I have shifted my entire relationship to the sun. I never got the skin rash ever again, either. And it was due to lifestyle changes, not a prescription.

We have been taught that the sun is our enemy. We have been taught that exposure to the sun will cause skin cancer. We have been taught to avoid the sun as much as possible. If we are outside, even just for a little while, we should protect ourselves from the sun's harmful rays with sunscreen. In addition, modern western life has all but removed the sun from most of our daily activities. We spend most of our lives indoors. We leave our houses by way of our vehicles and quickly enter another building, be it school, work, appointments, or after hours activities. We spend most of our lives not in sunlight, but, rather, bathed in the artificial light of bulbs and staring at screens of one type or another. When we leave the house, it is more like we are entering a foreign world. If we are outside for mere moments, we cover ourselves in synthetic sunscreen.

Conventional thinking has you avoiding and protecting yourself from the sun at all costs. I am constantly reprimanded by others for my perceptions of the positivity of sun exposure. In her book: *Renegade Beauty*, Nadine Artemis tells a narrative in which the sun has been demonized in modern times. Yet the sun itself, as little as a hundred years ago, was used to cure diseases and make strong and healthy humans.

Artemis explains how Vitamin D is a steroid hormone that benefits every organ and cell in the body and even boosts immunity. The true source of usable Vitamin D is from the rays of the sun. It is like a magic ingredient that bolsters all bodily functions and seeps its way into every part of you. It is essential for unlocking numerous genes for access to your vitality. In addition, our skin is actually designed like a solar panel to take in the energy of the sun, and applying a sunscreen disrupts how you receive those loving and beneficial rays. The sun is good for your skin and is an antiseptic. It improves your mood and also tones muscles without exercising.

Our friend, the Sun, the provider of the energy for all life on our planet is especially important to those suffering from depression. It may be just the remedy that is missing for you. Remember we are taking the holistic approach here, one that looks at the whole body. How could something that has so many benefits not affect your mood?

In his book, *The Depression Cure*, Stephen S. Ilardi, PhD also emphasizes the importance of sun exposure and vitamin D. He claims that Vitamin D is essential for almost all bodily functions and a deficiency can lead to all sorts of diseases. The appropriate amount of time to expose yourself to the sun is the same amount that it takes to get the slightest hint of a tan. The following examples are for a person in a swimsuit where most of your body is exposed. From May to August he advocates for ten to fifteen minutes a day of full sun exposure between 11:00 a.m. and 3:00 p.m. In March, April, September, and October he recommends 30 minutes per day. For those with a dark complexion, he recommends doubling those amounts of time.

I have my own personal approach. What follows are my personal strategies on how to reintroduce sunshine into your life. These tips are specifically for dwellers in the temperate zone of the Northern Hemisphere. Those in the Southern Hemisphere can easily reconfigure the time windows. When you are ready to take this on, I recommend doing it mindfully, gently, and effectively. If you haven't been in the sun in years and you decide to go outside all day with your shirt off, you will get burned and hurt yourself very badly. Please be safe and slow about your new relationship with the sun, or you'll get burned! You may even begin to plan your life for those ideal times of day to seek light and heat.

Disclaimer: You must be responsible to monitor and regulate your exposure to the sun. This includes the time of day, time of year, and amount of time per session. You must be the one who knows how much is too much. Please start slowly and build up your tolerance over time.

Strategy number one begins by dividing the year into two 6-month periods. The first period is between the Fall Equinox and the Spring Equinox, approximately mid-September to mid-March. For our purposes, let's say winter. I get out as much as I can during the middle of the day, from the hours of about 10 a.m. to 2 p.m. Here in the Denver metro area, where I live, we typically get frequent daytime temperatures as high as the 50's, Fahrenheit, where I can go shirtless and soak up as many rays as possible. If you can't take the cold yet at least get some sunshine on your face and hands. The second period is approximately mid-March to mid-September or the spring equinox to the autumn equinox. Let's say summer. This is a period of the most light and heat. I aim to get outside and get full sun before 10 a.m. or after 3 p.m., when the sun is not so strong and won't quickly cause a burn. This approach can vary depending on the exact time of year, your location, and how far along you are in your re-exposure journey. As for me after the better part of a decade using this technique, I can handle quite a bit of noontime light, even though my skin is naturally very fair.

The next strategy is for times that you find yourself outside all day during the summer months. Procure some very light and breathable materials for pants and a long-sleeved shirt. Also, acquire a large brimmed hat. Wear these during the sunniest and hottest hours of the day, typically between 10 a.m. and 3 p.m. These accessories will adequately protect you from burning during the most dangerous interval. You may be thinking, "Won't I be too hot?" Here's a tip. Completely saturate your shirt and pants in cold water until they are soaking wet. Put them back on and feel relief as you now have your very own built-in swamp cooler. Once when I was harvesting vegetables for a local organic farm in one hundred degree heat, I used this method and was happily shivering and cold while everyone else was miserably hot.

The last strategy is especially important for those of you who are just starting out after a long period of lack of exposure. There are some excellent skin protectors. My personal preference is shea butter. I have slathered my whole body on a cloudless Colorado day for a music festival, and at day's end, my skin was slightly pink. I did not suffer painful sunburn. Extra virgin coconut oil is another alternative. Both of these have great health benefits for your skin, like moisturizing, without causing permanent harm. Last, raspberry seed oil is the most comprehensive skin covering, making it great for newcomers. Remember that skin is the largest organ and absorbs a lot of what gets put on it. These options work with your natural biology, instead of against it like chemical sunscreens. One of my great inspirations, Arthur Haines, a multi-skilled naturalist, says don't put anything on your skin that you wouldn't eat.

In addition, in Chapter 7: "Let There Be Light," of Artemis' book, she explains that the many benefits of sun exposure are not achieved if one is wearing sunglasses. She says we absorb the light into our eyes and that also is extremely beneficial to well-being and happiness. I am WARNING you here to take this process slowly, and it is your choice. You will only hurt yourself if you go too fast with all or nothing thinking. And, no I am not advocating staring directly into the sun.

***There is a practice called sun gazing which you may research on your own and I will likely write about at another time, but it is not a subject for THIS book. Please don't stare into the sun. It's enough to be outside without sunglasses at different times of the day.

At this point, I only use eye protection during the day when the sun is shining after fresh snow as the reflection is too great. I'll also use eye protection when I am driving in the morning or evening and the angle of the sun is blinding me and affecting my ability to see to drive. If you are used to wearing sunglasses all the time then you must do this gradually. Begin by taking your glasses off for a few minutes a day only, then increase a few minutes at a time. Do not go to the point where your eyes hurt or strain. You must be responsible. In addition, if you have eye issues you must consult with your eye doctor. He or she may disagree with me. You are the decision-maker and the one in charge of your health. That is all I will say about that. Do not hurt yourself, as you have been warned multiple times.

In his book, Ilardi also supports this theory by stating the light of a sunny day is far brighter than artificial lighting and our eyes are made for being outside. There are unique receptors for light connected to the brain that only respond to the natural bright light of the sun. The outdoor light stimulates serotonin which again is critical for enhanced moods and behavior. Serotonin has an anti-depressive effect which can happen more quickly than with medications, he says. His case studies reveal that increased mood and well-being can be felt within hours or even minutes of sun exposure. He even goes on to say that when deprived of ample bright natural light our bodily functions deteriorate quickly and can actually cause depression. For those with seasonal depression, 30 minutes of sunlight exposure per day can be enough to alleviate depression, especially when combined with social interaction and exercise, both mentioned previously.

Part B: The False Glow

> We and everything else alive, from plankton and fungus to elephants and ants, are synchronized to the orbit and rotation of the earth in and out of the sun's light to assure us a food supply. All things great and small have internal sundials that measure time with molecular clocks in every cell that switch enormous cadres of regulatory genes on and off... There is an ever-churning circulating flow of energy driven by the light (Wiley 30).

From 2006 until 2010 I spent the majority of my time in New Zealand. Most of that period was in a little-known place called the Marlborough Sounds. It's located on the northeast tip of the South Island, an area where ancient river beds (now saltwater) meet small mountains. The area contains lush regrowth forest and scattered sheep farms the border turquoise ocean inlets. I was an hour and a half drive from the nearest stoplight, and it was sparsely populated with "batches," or summer cabins. If you traveled even further down a winding road that quickly turned into gravel and dirt, you'd come to where it ended at the open sea. To me, it seemed like I was in fairytale and this was the end of the world.

In such a rural area there were few people and little light pollution. Giant wild pigs, deer, and goats were the large animals to be heard and rarely seen. An amazing canopy featured many beautiful types of trees, birds, insects, and flowers. Most days from spring to fall I could swim in the sea 100 yards from my back door or from numerous little coves and inlets. In the winter it rained and was cold but never freezing. That time of my life was paradise.

The only Internet was dial-up and, while you could order satellite television, I chose not to bother after the first few months. I was finally out living deep in nature, which I love. As I had few screens to look at except for the occasional e-mail, and an old flip phone, I soon found myself venturing outside at night without the help of any flashlight. It was amazing. On a moonlit night, I could see very well and navigate narrow trails unscathed. I could see well enough when there were only stars, even if I had to move a bit slower. I couldn't believe the abilities of sight that returned to me once I didn't have the option to watch TV and stare at computer screens all day. It was as if I had the night vision of an owl.

Everything else on Earth except for us honors the cycles of nature. Other animals live and die by the seasons. They do not have a choice. We have created numerous ways to separate ourselves from the cycles of this planet.

In the book, *Lights Out: Sleep, Sugar, and Survival*, by T.S. Wiley, the author presents a narrative in which our departure from the cycles of nature has had devastating effects on our health. He points out how the creation of artificial light has extended our days and ruined our health. Most of today's health issues started with the altering of the light cycle.

Unless you live right on the equator, then there is some variance of daylight a human will receive throughout the year. Most of the population lives in temperate climates and sees huge shifts in the amount of daylight received at particular locations from summer to winter in a year. This is a part of how all nature operates, outside of ourselves. The never-ending day has allowed us the opportunity to alter our sleep cycles and we never truly experience the seasons anymore.

We are now living artificial lives. Artificial light has created artificial living. Most of us spend the majority of our time indoors. We are under artificial light even during the day in buildings and schools and finally in our homes. There are not many people I know who let the sun shine in, even leaving the shades mostly drawn during the day so that it doesn't put a glare on the television screen or closing the curtains for privacy.

Then, at the slightest hint of dark, we turn on the brightest light in the house so we can see for all the other night activities. Mealtime, homework, and watching television...it never ends. When exercising at the gym or going to an event at night you will be blasted by bright fluorescent lights. We have altered the day to meet our desires. Even if you have the lights off or dim you are likely staring at a screen for hours into the night. Just what has this done and what is this doing to us?

Most of us don't even consider this could have an effect on our health, mood, and well-being. How did we lose our way? We do so by continuing to just accept the next big technological thing as the proper thing to do. Lightbulbs, sure why not. Television, fantastic. A phone (really a computer) that I can find entertainment on and stare all the time. Yes, please! We have either not thought about it at all or if we have, we are not willing to give up convenience and entertainment for our health.

Coming from a holistic perspective how does this connect to depression? Considering the entire being, this denial of the seasonal cycle alters sleep, hormones, mood, appetite, and more. With no connection to the natural time clock of days, months, years, and so on, our species is suffering from an epidemic of obesity and disease that manifests in so many ways. For a lot of us, these imbalances also may occur as depression.

It's time to take steps to protect your eyes and skin from overexposure to fluorescent bulbs during the hours of dark and wear blue-light-blocking glasses at night when lights are on or staring at the screens. You can purchase very inexpensive blue-blocking glasses or more expensive stylish ones. Some companies can even install prescription lenses if required. This book is being completed in 2019, and there are options for blue-light-blocking glasses and all other kinds of products now. With simple Internet searches, you can find every product you are seeking, even ones not presented here.

Your computer phone likely comes with a blue light-blocking feature for nighttime or you can easily download an app for free or minimal cost. I have also found that red light bulbs can reduce the eye problems at night as they allow me to see what I need to do but don't disrupt my night vision or cause my body to think that it is mid-day when it's nighttime.

Why do this? Why go against the mainstream here? If you value your well-being and desire to reduce your depressive symptoms, then it is worth it. Nature is always waiting right outside. She reminds us who is truly in charge, despite our technology and ability to control the light. When things get out of balance, nature will correct it. I have tried and tested everything I recommend so I know that I am giving you the best information I have at this time.

Chapter 9: The Healing Powers of Earth

Part A: Earthing

"Most of us Tramp through the world having forgotten we are a part of it" (Wiley 33).

In the United States of America and other Westernized nations we have mostly lost our connection with the Earth, our mother. The Earth provides all. Can you name any product that the Earth did not have a part in making? Today, most of us are nearly completely physically disconnected. We stay inside our homes, and go directly to our cars, from the cars back to inside buildings. Then we go back to the cars, and then back inside our houses. Those of us that make it a point to go outside each day or be in nature are most likely to do so in synthetic shoes. One of the only exceptions may be if you are a home gardener or small farmer who doesn't wear gloves and occasionally shifts some dirt with your hands.

Inflammation is the culprit in most cases of depression, especially those depressions not brought upon by grief, according to Kelly Brogan, MD, with Kristin Loberg in their book *A Mind of Your Own*. In this book, Dr. Brogan, a psychiatrist, clearly demonstrates that chronic inflammation is a result of our modern lifestyles—those that are stressful, in which we are sedentary, and where there is an absence of real food. She focuses her view away from the brain chemistry theory on the impact of chronic inflammation caused by modern living. I have shown over and over in this book how modern living is far from how our species is designed to live. Some inflammation is okay and the sign of a healthy immune system. But when our bodies are never allowed to heal, that inflammation becomes chronic.

Furthermore, in their book *Earthing: The Most Important Health Discovery Ever*, by Clinton Ober, Stephen T. Sinatra, and Martin Zucker, the authors reiterate that inflammation is the underlying culprit to more than eighty chronic illnesses. They provide a significant solution to inflammation, called *earthing*, which they define as "living in contact with Earth's natural surface charge--being grounded--which naturally discharges and prevents chronic inflammation in the body."

Simply put, their premise is the ground contains a negative frequency. In modern life, we are subjected to constant positive frequencies from our mobile phones, electronics, and pseudo-foods, and much more. We also tend to store up this massive positive charge that results in inflammation, the cause of most illness and disease. Touching the Earth directly ground us. We release positive charges and absorb negative charges, balancing and restoring harmony to ourselves.

This book documents how reconnecting and grounding the body consistently produces these and other common benefits:

- Rapid reduction of inflammation
- Rapid reduction or elimination of chronic pain

- Dynamic blood flow improvement to better supply the cells and tissues of the body with vital oxygen and nutrition
- Reduced stress
- Increased energy
- Improved sleep
- Accelerated healing from injuries and surgery

Earthing can be a significant holistic treatment for depression, as its greatest benefit is reducing inflammation. In addition, according to Ober, Sinatra, and Zucker, *earthing* can assist with stabilizing serotonin levels. Serotonin is the main chemical that most antidepressant pharmaceuticals are trying to balance according to the chemical imbalance theory. Serotonin assists with decreasing crying spells, near-tearful-ness, and obsessive/repetitive negative thoughts. When depression symptoms lessen, energy levels rise and tolerance to stressful situations, pain and discomfort improves.

Getting started is as simple as taking off your shoes and spending more time barefoot and in contact with the bare earth. Even laying in the park on a blanket is enough. After realizing the tremendous benefits of this practice, I made my own *earthing* mat from materials at the hardware store.

I sleep on my *earthing* mat at night so that I am spending almost a third of my time harmonizing my frequency and reducing inflammation. You too can create a do-it-yourself mat with a simple internet search. For more information or to purchase ready-made and easy to use products, please visit www.earthing.com.

Part B: Barefoot Warriors of Peace

Almost a decade ago, I took off my shoes and never looked back. I realized that no other animal in this world wore coverings on their appendages to protect their hands, feet, hoofs, paws, etc. I looked at my hands and thought, what would happen to them if I were to put socks and shoes on my hands each day. Wouldn't their performance decrease over a period of time? Wouldn't the muscles atrophy and the functionality disappear? Our feet have the second-highest number of nerve endings in our bodies after our sexual organs. They were designed to navigate a variety of surfaces and communicate with our brains. As I spent more time outside with my bare feet connected to the ground, I noticed an overall sense of calm and happiness. What I didn't know then is that the increased hours of bare skin contact with the earth was gently harmonizing my body and boosting my well-being and happiness.

My feet were crammed into shoes that were too small. My feet were imprisoned. My parents weren't rich, but we weren't poor either. I'd say I grew up in the lower middle class. I had hand-me-down's from my brother, and probably got new sized shoes a little too late. During my formative years, my feet were deformed like everyone else's, my pinky toes smashed into the confinement of shoes.

This affects the way you stand and walk. How can we ever have correct postures if we stuff our feet into shoes? I think the injuries I've sustained have a lot to do with this. If my feet were stuffed into shoes then that would misalign my bones from my ankles to my shins, then my knees and on up to my spine shoulders and neck.

In Chapter 25 of the book *Born to Run: A Hidden Tribe, Superathletes, and the Greatest Race the World Has Never Seen*, author Christopher McDougall presents three painful truths:

> Painful truth #1 - The Best Shoes are the Worst: Studies are finding that wearers of expensive running shoes that are promoted as having additional features that protect (e.g., more cushioning, 'pronation correction') are injured significantly more frequently than those wearing inexpensive running shoes.

> Painful truth #2 - Feet Like a Good Beating: Studies from mega giant Nike itself show that the added cushioning in shoes does nothing to lessen impact. It actually INCREASES it. The more cushioned the shoe, the less protection it provides.

> Painful Truth #3 - Human Beings were Designed to Run without Shoes: Dr. Gerard Hartmann, P.T., the Irish physical therapist who serves at the Great and Powerful Oz for the world's finest distance runners. "The deconditioned musculature of the foot is the greatest issue leading to injury, and we've allowed our feet to become badly deconditioned over the past few decades."

These same concepts about running shoes can be applied to any activity, especially walking, and your daily routines. On the webpage for The Society for Barefoot Living, it says,

The fact is, human feet were designed for walking barefoot, and they continue to be totally efficient and sufficient for that purpose.... Though feet tend to remain soft and weak with regular shoe wearing, they will – like any other part of the body – grow stronger, healthier and more resilient when allowed to function as nature intended: moving freely, and exposed to fresh air and sunlight while unencumbered by tight restraints (shoes).

So, what can you do? First, take your shoes off indoors and be barefoot for your daily activities. Also, begin to walk around outside in the soft grass of your yard or a nearby park. After a while, you can experiment with hard surfaces, like rock beds and trails. Be mindful and gradual as there are countless hazards, and your feet are most likely weak and soft. Even after almost six years of dedication it still hurts when I step on a thorn or sharp stick. The benefits far exceed the occasional minor impairment.

A strategy I live by is to always be as close to barefoot as I can. There are now numerous brands of footwear that cater to us barefoot warriors. They recognize the need for a flat shoe and wide toe box, allowing the foot to sit more naturally. Simply search "barefoot shoes" or "minimalist footwear" in your favorite search engine.

Some added bonuses I experience are that I can now withstand very cold temperatures and even walk around in the snow for longer and longer periods of time. My feet are simultaneously becoming tougher and more sensitive to touch. Your foot strength and, perhaps more importantly, your overall health will improve. Being barefoot as often as possible not only opens you up to earthing in a natural way but also can correct posture and chronic pain or injury.

Resources:

https://www.earthing.com/

www.barefooters.com

https://www.thebarefootrunners.org/

Chapter 10: Hygiene as Nourishment

Over the course of a year, I weaned myself off the use of shampoo. I had done some research and decided that the best things to use were aluminum-free baking soda to wash and pure apple cider vinegar to condition my hair. I began to stretch out the days between uses. At first, my hair was greasy. For a while, I used baking soda and apple cider vinegar every three days. Then, once a week. Then, once every two weeks. Then, once a month. It took me about a year to get to once a month where my hair didn't appear greasy. Over the course of the next few years, I only needed to clean my hair every 3 months or so. After the shampoo experiment, I began to employ the same concept with every type of product sold to us as a must for modern life. Today I live with almost no purchased hygiene products. The exceptions I use are purely sourced and made. They do not affect my well-being with harmful substances. We live in an age where certain handpicked products can even boost your overall vitality.

The vast majority of hygiene products, even so-called natural ones, contain substances that are harmful. Today's essential mainstream products include toothpaste, shampoo, soap, conditioner, moisturizer, make-up, sunscreen, household cleaners, and more. We are agreeing to surround ourselves, bathe, apply, and even ingest harmful synthetic ingredients. The best thing we can do for ourselves today is to throw them all in the trash and start over.

Let's replace the word clean with the word sterile. A sterile environment is the breeding ground for disease. Think again of the microbiome. We already discussed what happens with sterile water and processed food. It's the same with conventional hygiene products. This has a detrimental effect on your overall well-being and the harmony of your ecosystem. This detrimental effect expresses itself as depression for some individuals. The impact is a toxicant overload. You are a machine. Your body and organs are designed to rid themselves of the bad stuff on their own. In the distant past, when we were living in a much more harmonious way with nature, it was no big deal. Our organs and body had no problem purifying itself because the environment was free of manmade substances. Yes, there were poisonous plants and mushrooms, but the tribes knew what those were and avoided them. In today's world, there are toxicants in the air you breathe, the water you drink and bathe in, the food you eat, the products you use, the cleaners used in homes and all buildings, really. It's everywhere. You can't escape. I've heard how they have found traces of pesticides in Antarctica. The earth is a closed system. What happens in one place happens everywhere.

The solution is to reduce to a minimum amount of these products that you use on your body and around you. Make choices for purity over sterility, and your body will have a chance to cleanse itself of unwanted materials. Our bodies, like every other animal, are perfectly capable of performing all its processes. There probably could be and most likely are entire books written on the hazards of modern cleaning products.

There are two ways to go about this process. The first is the path I chose which is completely clearing my environment of all conventional products, be they for hygiene or cleaning. By removing all questionable products, my body became free to come back into harmony. I may smell from time to time, but the positive result is I haven't had the common cold or seasonal flu in over a decade. I have found that I smelled much worse when my body had to process all the synthetic ingredients in the products themselves.

Path number two is to completely overhaul your products. This is likely the way that most will choose. I understand you probably have jobs and must keep up appearances and smell nice or not smell at all. Here is how to go about this. Throw away all conventional products and replace them with pure options. If you are not currently experiencing extreme symptoms, the weaning process can be done gently and mindfully over time. Give yourself a chance to adjust gradually and avoid the shock to your physical and mental state of giving up everything at once.

What is a pure product? A pure product is produced from start to finish with your utmost health, and the health of the plants, etc. that made the product in mind. With products free of all artificial and synthetic ingredients there is nothing to detox. Not only are these products neutral, but, relying on natural herbs and oils, they can actually work with the body to expedite wellness. I cannot stress enough that we live in a time where this is actually available. All products can be replaced, and you can choose to nourish yourself inside and out.

We live in an amazing time. Most health stores and natural food stores contain much better options for your hygiene and cleaning products than mainstream stores. You don't have to be a scientist to figure it out, but you must learn to become a label reader or friends with the clerks at the store. Avoid anything with petroleum byproducts and synthetic sounding names. Look for products with the least amount of ingredients. A simple search on the internet on your favorite search engine will likely result in a variety of choices. You will learn to be discerning in finding the purest products. While they often cost a bit more, you also use a lot less each time in general. Let go of the desire for every product to become foamy or have a strong fake smell as an indication of cleanliness. You won't regret it. As a result, your body will function optimally, as it's designed to do, and your depressive symptoms will continue to lessen.

Sidebar #4: Oral Health

Dental and oral health is a vastly underrated part of the equation of optimizing your overall and mental health. Unfortunately, in the year of the writing of this book, 2019, conventional dentistry still uses highly questionable methods and substances. To review the misuse of fluoride, please see Chapter 4, "The Water of Life". Many tooth-filling materials contain elemental (metallic) mercury. Fillings containing this substance are known as amalgams. According to the International Academy of Oral Medicine and Toxicology, or IAOMT, there is ample evidence of links between mental illness (depression, anxiety, and suicide) and amalgam fillings. Also, the root canal as an effective procedure is under debate about the long-term effects. Personally, I choose to have my own oral health under the supervision of progressive biodentistry. I have had all of my amalgam fillings removed and replaced. As a result, I no longer feel chronic fatigue. Although I have had to have a few teeth extracted due to decay, I have never had a root canal, and I will never ever go that route. To reverse the procedures and methods of conventional dentistry was one of the best decisions I have ever made for my overall well-being and vitality. It could be just the thing that is holding you back from your full potential as well.

Chapter 11: Seeking Holistic Care

My digestion hadn't been that great for as long as I could remember. I was either gassy or constipated or both. This is not a good way to feel all the time. After years overseas, my diet had changed quite a bit. The quality and quantity of foods available in America is unique in that the amount of choices of huge portions of pseudo food is always an option. I was as constipated as I had ever been, not being able to properly use the bathroom for months. I tried all the conventional over the counter stuff: psyllium husk, over the counter pooping pills, etc. Nothing worked and I felt awful. I was putting on weight and my mood was miserable. I began to dread eating because it seemed that I was never going to evacuate again. This issue also significantly increased the depressive episode I was going through at the time.

Finally, after months of suffering, I was willing to do anything, and I had my first visit with a naturopathic doctor. I was shocked that the appointment lasted three hours as the professional guided me through a step-by-step questionnaire and multiple other tests. Given the extreme nature of the problem I was having, the doctor recommended three things to start. First, I would come in for three rounds of colon hydrotherapy to cleanse a dysfunctional digestive tract and remove stagnant waste. Second, I was to eliminate certain foods from my diet that, according to the symptoms, she thought were exacerbating the problem. Third, I was to trial a homeopathy regimen as a remedy to the severe depressive moods I was experiencing.

While there were some adjustments along the way with the treatments, I am happy to say that my digestion returned to mostly normal, and the depressive moods did lighten considerably. I also lost a good amount of weight from eating a better diet.

There is more than a choice between modern Western medicine and alternatives. There are three traditions of healing.

Susan Weed, an herbalist, a researcher, and author describes the three traditions of healing that have developed over time: the *scientific*, the *heroic*, and the *wise woman* tradition. The *scientific* is congruent with allopathic medicine we know today. Ever wonder why there is a foot doctor, a heart doctor, a skin doctor, a joint doctor, and an eye doctor, among many others? Modern western treatment breaks the body down into parts and pieces, individual neurotransmitters, organs, and the like. This way creates symptoms and diagnoses so that the practitioner can address what's wrong in a certain area of the body.

The first path is called the *wise woman* or the *wisdom* tradition. This is the holistic perspective and says that we are always in a state which is whole, perfect, and complete. When something is wrong, or and illness or disease appears, then the practitioner looks at the entire being for answers, not just a part of the body. He or she investigates the physical, mental, emotional, and spiritual as one being and looks for which part is not being nourished enough or is being neglected.

The *wise woman* tradition, focusing on integration and nourishment, and insisting on attention to uniqueness and holographic interconnectedness is a new way that is also the most ancient healing way known. A way that follows a spiral path, a give-away dance of nourishment, change, and self-love. "Trust yourself" is the message here.

The second modality of healing is called the *heroic* tradition. This way looks at the physical body as lower than the mental/emotional that is lower than the spirit. Physical matter is the lowest form of consciousness. In this model, the body and environment are dirty and must be constantly cleansed and cleaned. The environment is full of toxicants and we must keep the body clean to interact with a higher version of ourselves. Alternative health care practitioners usually think in the *heroic* tradition: the way of the savior, a circular path of rules, punishment, and purification. "Trust Me."

AMA-approved, legal, covered-by-insurance health care practitioners are trained to think in the *scientific* tradition: walking the knife-edge of keen intellect; the straight line of analytical thought; measuring and repeating and, measuring and repeating is excellent for fixing broken things. "Trust my machine."

The *scientific*, *heroic*, and *wise woman* traditions are ways of thinking, not acting. Any practice, any technique, any substance can be used by a practitioner/helper in any of the three traditions... The same techniques, the same herbs are seen and used differently by a person thinking in scientific, heroic, or wise woman ways (Weed 1).

After my personal experiences and the testimonies of others, I think that the scientific allopathic, or modern conventional medicine, has way overstepped its authority. Western methods are certainly a miracle in emergencies. If I get shot or stabbed or run over or my heart stops, I want to go to the hospital. If I need surgery in an emergency, then modern medicine is the miracle I need. However, when they apply this methodology to all symptoms and illnesses, it creates a modern health crisis. All illnesses and diseases, including depression and suicide, are rampant and on the rise despite our advances in technologies and numerous pharmaceuticals. As I have shown earlier, they even make up illnesses so that there is something to diagnose and fix and to placate the pharmaceutical companies.

Before I begin to describe some alternatives let me say that what I am about to share is only the tip of the iceberg when it comes to alternative healing modalities. There are many options that have easily filled up books on their own. The purpose of this book is merely to point you in a new direction and give you places to start. How a new path develops for you is entirely up to you and the choices you make. What I will say is that expectations of what will and won't work, or how it should or is supposed to go will hinder you in this process. Also, in order for any of these modalities to work it takes follow-through on your part. If you go to a naturopath and don't follow any of their instructions, then you can't say it didn't work. The new way takes your full participation and requires you to make necessary changes to your lifestyle.

In addition, if you come into this process looking to be cured, you may be sorely disappointed. Conventional medicine is rife with the next cure. The mentality of a diagnosis that says something is wrong and needs to be fixed then breaks the human being into parts and pieces won't lead to a cure for many of these lifestyle type illnesses like depression. The alternatives I recommend dance in the grey area between the wisdom path and the heroic path. It has been shown in previous chapters that our environments are indeed full of toxicants and poisons. While harsh cleanses and detoxes may not be necessary unless things get to an emergency state, it is gentle lifestyle changes over time that will make the most difference for you.

Doing this all on your own is possible, but not recommended. Connection with other humans is obviously important. Trusting someone to help you by utilizing their talents and skills will lessen your symptoms exponentially. It's true that I researched and implemented a lot of changes on my own. You can, too. In the anecdote at the beginning of this chapter, I finally began to rely on the assistance of other practitioners. They won't necessarily fix you, but the application of their expertise allows you to heal. They believe you can restore yourself to your birthright of well-being, and their methods will help get you there. Let go of doing it all alone and seek as much assistance as you can along the way.

There are so many means of alternative assistance beyond western medicine that I can't relay them all, but here are some: naturopaths, body talk, acupuncture, homeopathy, herbalism, shamanism, holistic health and wellness coaches, all kinds of massage and bodywork, cranial-sacral therapy, and more. My recommendation is to find one or more that can guide you along your journey. Those people will likely change as you grow into your true healthy self.

The first stop could be a naturopath, holistic doctor, or holistic health coach. This approach looks at the whole being, including mental, emotional, spiritual, and physical aspects. Most of the approaches here are gentle and non-invasive, seeking to assist the individual in healing themselves. Within the naturopath's tool kit are many methods of healing. Note that some naturopaths may differ in their exact techniques, so it is good to find one that you connect with and are willing to do what they say. It's important that you feel comfortable and safe. I want to offer you just a few options where you can begin your own healing journey.

Energy healing seeks to work on the invisible and non-physical aspects of the human being. Human auras have been measured since the 1950s. The physical and energetic are all connected so the physical malady will also be found within the energy body. Shamanism is the oldest modality of healing on Earth. Images of the disheveled loner deep in the wilderness casting spells and chanting come to mind. Modern shamans come in all shapes, colors, and sizes and could have trained for years or just a weekend. You must take care to find one with whom you resonate. They work in the world of energy and spirit to find the imbalance within the energy body. Once the energy body is restored, the healing works its way through, eventually, to the physical body.

Homeopathy is a modality that is often utilized by naturopaths and holistic doctors. In homeopathy, a plant or substance is identified that causes the same symptoms or reactions that you are having. That substance or plant is then broken down and distilled over and over again until there is no trace of the original substance. The theory here is that "like cures like", and in the treatment, only the energy of the like substance is left as there is no physical trace. Flower essences are another energy treatment used for millennia. It is a similar concept to homeopathy, but certain flower essences can be used to boost mood as a remedy for what ails you.

Herbalism is the ancient practice of using plants to heal and treat disease. It can also be used to boost the well-being of someone who isn't experiencing symptoms of illness. Practitioners go to school to learn about the physical and energetic properties of plants that have been used as treatments for centuries. Herbs are full of the very micronutrients that are deficient in modern diets that are already lacking a variety of plants. The majority of herbalists use at least organic and sometimes wild-crafted plants to make their concoctions. Herbal teas are only one way to ingest the necessary dosages of mood-improving plants. When the body is nourished then how could you not feel better?

Essential oils take this a step further and are highly concentrated oils made from plants. Often it takes a large amount of plant material to make a single drop of oil. Again, these remedies have been used for a long time to treat maladies and improve moods. Unlike conventional treatments, plant oils used properly work in harmony with the body and boost the processes already existing in the body itself.

Acupuncture is based on the Chinese energy system in the body. All bodies are said to have the same energy system that can be stimulated with needles in specific points. The theory goes that energy channels become stagnant for a variety of reasons. Small needles are used to stimulate the channels through specific points. Find the right practitioner and learn to relax and enjoy because the visit can often lead to a very relaxed state. Multiple visits are usually necessary. Once you are stable, routine maintenance is recommended.

Body Talk is a non-invasive type of energy work. The whole body and whole being is assessed versus specific aches, pains, issues, etc. A truly holistic approach, the practitioners are trained to listen to the urgent needs of your body, versus what you think may need at the time. Body Talk utilizes tapping and gentle breathing to reconnect areas of your body that have lost communication due to injury, trauma, or stress. Your body tells a story of all the things that have occurred in your life, positive and negative, as well as what you've inherited from family, genetics, and so on. The practitioner helps to bring awareness to what's going on inside and around you and also education on how to correct current imbalances. Body Talk is one of my personal favorite forms of Holistic care.

Conclusion

You have just read my story. My own journey began with a series of traumatic childhood events that led to the distrust of others and isolation. I developed numerous unhealthy patterns of overeating, checking out through an endless supply of Hollywood programming, and drinking alcohol, among other things.

In my late teens and early twenties, I was diagnosed and treated by western medicine for recurring and worsening episodes of depression. I spent much of that time hoping for death and ruminating on suicide almost every day. According to western doctors, I had a lifelong illness due to a chemical imbalance in my brain that could only be corrected with pharmaceutical drugs. A managed life was the best I could hope for, they said.

I rebelled against their prognosis. It took a lot of time, research, effort, and implementation to escape the misery of depression. I did it, though, and people who meet me today can hardly believe that I was at one time suicidal and one hundred pounds heavier. It is not an easy path I chose, but I am a healthier and confident human being as a result.

I no longer suffer from depressive episodes or disappear from the world. I embody all of the ways of being, techniques, and strategies from this book. I participate in numerous communities for human connection and growth. I consume pure water and food. I practice various movement styles to stay strong and mobile. I let myself be nourished by the sun's brilliant rays as much as possible. I walk barefoot on the earth and sleep on a homemade grounding mat each night. I avoid contaminated hygiene products and I regularly meet with holistic practitioners to help guide me. This is a new way. You can have it too with simple changes to your lifestyle over time.

Is my life perfect? No. Am I always happy? Nope. Do I stumble on my path? Yes. Will you stumble on your path? Likely, yes, and you will now have some tools in your toolbox to help you along the way. Depressive moods are a natural part of the human experience of life. When the experience is prolonged and pronounced it is a big clue that your physical body is not functioning properly. Now you have a handful of ways to change that. I hope that you do! I wish you well on your journey. Thank you for being a part of mine.

Resources:

1. Artemis, Nadine (2017) *Renegade Beauty: Reveal and Revive Your Natural Radiance.* Berkley, CA: North Atlantic Books.

2. Artemis, Nadine (2013) *Holistic Dental Care: The Complete Guide to Healthy Teeth and Gums.* Berkley, CA: North Atlantic Books.

3. Brogan, Kelly, MD, with Kristin Loberg (2016) *A Mind of Your Own: The Truth About Depression and How Women Can Heal Their Bodies to Reclaim Their Lives.* New York, NY: HarperCollins.

4. Hawkins, David R. MD and PhD (2012) *Letting Go: The Pathway to Surrender.* Carlsbad, CA: Hay House, Inc.

5. Ilardi, Stephen S., PhD (2009) *The Depression Cure: The 6-Step Program to Beat Depression Without Drugs.* Cambridge, MA: Da Capo Press.

6. McDougall, Christopher (2009) *Born to Run: A Hidden Tribe, Superathletes, and the Greatest Race the World Has Never Seen.* New York, NY: Vintage Books.

7. Ober, Clinton, Sinatra, MD, Stephen T., and Zucker, Martin (2014) *Earthing: The Most Important Health Discovery Ever!* Laguna Beach, CA: Basic Health Publication, Inc.

8. Weed, Susun S. (1989) *Wise Woman Herbal: Healing Wise.* Woodstock, NY: Ash Tree Publishing.

9. Whitaker, Robert, and Cosgrove, Lisa (2015) *Psychiatry Under the Influence: Institutional Corruption, Social Injury, and Prescriptions for Reform.* New York, NY: Palgrave Macmillan.

10. Wiley, T. S., & Formby, PhD, Bent (2014) *Lights Out: Sleep, Sugar, and Survival.* New York, NY: Atria Paperback.